3-22-2019
what a grand and g[...] !

James),
Enjoy a copy [...]
& share with someone w[...]
need the tools to get out of
their Horror of a situation.

I hope you consider my book in Warwicks.
What else is possible and howmuch better
can it get than this?

Create Amazing Things!

[signature]

Jillian Coburn
Lago Vista, Texas

Cover Design: Migzworks
Editing-Interior Layout: The Self-Publishing Maven
Formatting: Chris Papapanagiotou

ISBN: 978-1-7335730-0-9
LCCN: 2019900850
Printed in the United States of America

MY UGLY TRUTH

LIFE BEYOND ABUSE

JILLIAN COBURN

ACKNOWLEDGMENTS

First, I acknowledge my husband for continuing to make me finish this book no matter how I felt. Without your encouragement and support, this book would not be possible.

I acknowledge my three children. Gabby your sparkle and drive make me want to continue to better myself because you are constantly reminding me what an amazing mom I am. To my two sons; Matthew and Lonnie, I pray that you treat your significant other with respect and love. One day I will let you read this book, and I hope you will see what abuse can look like and how women can suffer from words we say or physically do to them.

I thank my best buddies back at home in Lafayette, Louisiana the 337! Thank you to my lovely CAJUN LADIES; Allysun Mire, Keisha Holmes, Katy McCormick, Ali Parker, Yvette Naquin, Brittnay LeBlanc, Jill and Jillian Judice, and AJ Hendricks, without you cheering me own and being behind me throughout this entire process I would not have completed it to its fullest! I can sit here and name all the of you by name, but you know who you are and know that you are so loved by me and will always remain close to my prayers and my heart. Y'all need to understand that I couldn't have gotten to where I am today without every single one of who has walked this journey with me. It was a long one, and it was a lot of hard work very humiliating and humbling at the same time. But my story isn't over, it's just beginning so stay tuned and never give up what you LOVE!

Thanks to my Texas pals, Lauren, Carissa, Kari, Michelle and Cricket.

To my dad, Robert Mark Edwards, thank you for showing me how to love so unconditionally! Thank you for showing me what forgiveness looks like and thank you for being the best dad a little girl could ever ask for. I am sorry you are not here to see the wonderful things I am creating all because you nurtured and loved me so much.

To my mother, Frances Castaneda Edwards, thank you for showing me what tough love is and what it means to grab your big girl panties! You have raised some powerful women and thank you for showing me how to pray!

To my dad's sisters! Thank you for showing me what Faith looks like. I am so blessed to have such amazing role models. Aunt Brenda, you are an angel! Thank you for my cousins. Aunt Jane, thank you for loving my dad so much! He loved you dearly! You are such a kind person...

To my mom's sisters! Thank you for showing me what strong women are and always tooting my horn. I am so lucky for all of you!

My friend Anne Harb, Lisa Russo, Erin Dolan, Jeannine Edwards, Amber Arceneaux and Father Many, thank you for always showing me the Godly way!

Joi Stanley Smith, thank you for always believing in me and making sure I am at my best. Every week I enjoy your coaching and telling me to show up no matter how life may look. You have helped me tremendously with business deals as well as me not being abused by people taking advantage of me. You do not realize how much you mean to me and will never be forgotten.

DEDICATION

My uncle Father Dan Edwards, The Flying Priest, no matter what, you were always real with me never sugar coating my bad behavior always standing up for me and showing me the right way. You are what judgment is not! Always conscious of what it is going on but never judging. Your spirit is contagious and potent. How lucky are we to be in your presence? You were always that great role model. Thank you for always having faith in me and always reminding me of the light I am. Your journey has not been an easy one, and I always remind myself when I am down that my life could be worst. You are a true testament of faith and if everyone knew of your journey and how you continue to walk it with a smile always preaching the good word always reminding everyone to repent that God is waiting for us to scream HELP~ away from this worldly life! Thank you for emphasizing never to settle but being love and kind. I love you, and I want you to know God loves you so much! I am so lucky to have you as my uncle!

This book is dedicated to that one scared girl who may be reading this book and asking HOW DO I GET OUT? Let my ray of sunshine and positivity leads you away from the darkness. This book is for you! Put your sunglasses on and get ready to shine!

CONTENTS

MY STORY

There is a saying, "Some things are taught, and some things are caught!" Throughout my years on this earth, I've been taught and caught up in a lot.

Please allow me to share some of what I've been taught before I take you back a bit to the early years of my life. I've been taught that "Abuse" comes in several forms. You will read more about the various forms as my story unfolds but for now, let's discuss some detailed descriptions of abuse. Abuse can be mental, monetary, physical, sexual, substance and even spiritual. Abuse can be subtle or outright aggressive. Mental abuse is when one person puts another person down so much that the receiver of the abuse begins to lose their identity. Monetary abuse is when one party is in full control of the money. That person will dictate and even deprive the other party from spending. Physical abuse is when one or both parties become combative with each other. Sexual abuse is when one party forces another to have non-consensual sex. Spiritual abuse is when someone uses their connection to God to control or take advantage of you. I've experienced all these abuses. I write this book today knowing that none of it was what God intended for me. I now know that before we're born, God already has our lives mapped out. However, once we get to a certain age of understanding who He is, we must also seek to find what He requires, but more on that later.

The youngest of three girls, I was born in Opelousas, Louisiana on December 1, 1981, to Robert and Frances Edwards who were devout Catholics all their lives. My parents married in 1978 in Carencro, Louisiana by my grandfathers' only brother, Father Roy Edwards. My momma had been married before but divorced that man because he beat her. My parents met in California, but my dad convinced her that life in the Deep South would be wonderful. He had a tight-knit family and wanted to live close to his parents. Opelousas was a small town where everybody knew everybody, and neighbors were like family. My father would often leave Louisiana for work. He was a lumber broker who traveled the west coast. His work afforded my mother the opportunity to stay home with us with the help of Mrs. Lori, Mrs. Mildred as well as our five aunts and uncles. All these people had a huge impact on my faith and helped with the foundation that I would later use.

It's interesting how your life can change in a moment. I was five years old. It was a hot summer day, and we were at the house as a family. My dad had mowed the lawn that day and took off his shirt like he always did. Later that evening we lay on the grass, we looked up at the shooting stars as he asked me about my day. As the night cooled off, we all went to bed. A few hours later, I was awakened to a loud scream and was told to stay in my room. My father had a massive heart attack, and our lives would be different from that point forward. My dad was only thirty-five, and he could no longer work. From then on, he stayed home while my mother went out to work.

At the age of seven, we moved to Lafayette, Louisiana so my mother could go back to school and support the family. I attended Cathedral Carmel School and St. Thomas More Catholic High School. It was the land of big oil rigs and a little bit of weird. It was hard seeing others have things that were much nicer than ours, but in so many ways our lives seemed perfect. We would spend every Easter and Fourth of July in Destin, Florida, Christmas and Thanksgiving in California. We attended mass every Sunday at my uncles' church, my parents would pray every single night, and we observed all Holy days.

Me, I must be honest and say that while I had the semi-perfect life, Jillian wasn't the perfect little girl. I was very insecure. Kids teased me about my skin tone. I have an olive complexion and dark hair while the other children were fair skinned and blonde. My dad would caution me to stay out of the sun because my skin would get very dark and the other kids would call me black. I was also bullied for my size; I was a chunky kid. By high school, I had had enough of being bullied and learned to bully others instead. You see, I was running with a fast girl named Linda who I thought was cool because she used drugs and ran with the older drug dealers. The truth is she flunked the fourth grade and was as mean as a rattlesnake. I had become one of the tough girls, and I enjoyed the status it brought me. My very first encounter with sex was at the age of fourteen or fifteen with a boy I knew from elementary school. I lied to my father and told him I was going to mass on Christmas Eve, so I could be with him. This first experience with sex was terrible, and I felt so bad lying to my father. I kept thinking I am surely going to hell. Looking back, I know my path is not what God intended, but it had to happen for me to get to this point of sharing my story with you. My dad would catch me getting into trouble. He would get angry and threaten me. I would just laugh at him and call him the incredible hulk. The issues I had with using dope and eating were never addressed and became out of control. In other words, there were no real consequences for my actions.

MY PATH OF BAD CHOICES

My first love was named Jacob. For me, it was love at first sight. Although he was my first love, I couldn't be with him because he was my friend's boyfriend. Instead, I was with Joshua, a sweet guy on the outside but really a psycho inside! The cycle of abuse had begun at the age of fifteen. I convinced myself I loved the psycho. We would go swimming, ride jet skis, and smoke weed while drinking alcohol in Butte La rose-East of Lafayette, Louisiana. Jacob and Joshua showed me what crack-cocaine looked like, but I didn't use it with them. One day, we had been on the water all day riding down the basin, cutting up, boozing, and popping pills. Remember I told myself I was in LOVE! After the long day, we loaded up the jet skis and stopped at the corner store in this small town. There was another couple with us, Brandon and Sky. We stopped and went inside the store with our nasty, muddy suits, and purchased some snacks. After leaving the store, my LOVE decided to get loud and threw a beer bottle at my face and lunged for me. Scared and frightened I began to cry, and my friend pulled him off me and almost beat the crap out of him. Of course, the corner store called the police, and he was arrested for public intoxication and domestic abuse. I remember crying and being so sad because he was going to jail. Let me stop now and tell you I honestly thought what he did was okay. He went to jail in St. Martin Parish, and they shipped him away to federal prison for other charges that were pending in other parishes.

I remember the first time I got caught in my drug mess. Now I was still fifteen years old wearing a pager and one day my father beeps me saying he needed me home now. You see, I was just snorting cocaine off a bathroom toilet. I absolutely freaked out and decided I would go to a place called Breaux Bridge to a pharmacy to get a detoxer. Of course, it didn't work! I get home coked out of my mind, and he immediately took me to the doctor and had them draw my blood. I tried to pitch a fit, but my father didn't have it. We went back for the results, and I was diagnosed with ADD/ADHD and given medication to treat it. However, I saw my medical records and realized I was only tested for cocaine, which was positive. In anger, I grabbed the medical records and put them in my purse. My parents didn't know what to do with me. My uncles and our priest found out about what I did with the paperwork and came to the house telling me that I needed to go to Jesus Camp to be with my real friends. I agreed and boarded the bus to Windy Gap Christian Camp. It didn't scare me straight like they hoped. I remember watching the other kids eat magic mushrooms and wishing I was back home

In all that I had done and put my parents through by hanging with the wrong crowd, getting high, having a new boyfriend every month, having sex and simply not giving a shit, I passed school with flying colors, managed to graduate from high school and was given my own apartment and car. There were never any consequences for my actions with my parents. I don't fault them; they simply didn't know what to do with me. My mother would leave every summer to visit her family and my sisters, and I stayed behind with my dad. As long as we weren't causing trouble, it was good. My mom often said that my dad was the one who would not give consequences.

At the age of 17, I was raped by a 25-year-old pharmacist who worked for a major drug store. It was date rape; I snorted a Roxy and passed out. I awakened to find him on top of me, and I screamed while my roommate was in the other room tripping on Molly. The next day I went to the hospital, had a rape kit and went on my way like it never happened. I took the morning after pill, went to Florida on a trip and came back. Once I returned, my life took an even more interesting turn. I began attending the University of Louisiana at Lafayette, and in the summer of my freshmen year, I met James. He was twenty-one, and my main attraction to him was because he had Pot and Xanax. We would go to the movies, hang out and have unprotected sex. After one month I was pregnant. I tried to have an abortion, but it didn't work out. We stopped seeing each other for a few months, and the following Valentine's Day he proposed to me. I remember it like it was yesterday, we were at a Mexican restaurant and I was wearing overalls. I hated the princess cut ring he gave, but I said yes because I was doing the right thing for our child. My Gabby was born 7lbs. 11oz that May and we were married that same year in July.

Truthfully, I didn't want to get married but wanted to stay in college. However, I felt the pressure of obligation for my daughter to be raised with both her parents and I didn't want to hurt his feelings. My mother wanted me to be sure because she felt I was too young for marriage.

The day of my wedding I was shaking like a leaf walking into the Catholic Church. I told my father that I was making a mistake and didn't want to go through with it. However, I had to pull myself together and move forward because I didn't want to disappoint him and my family. We had great examples of people being married or a long time around us, so we fantasized about being together for 50 years. Our so-called honeymoon was a disaster. Traveling, he was drinking, drugging and passing out. Another cycle begins.

There were several reasons why we should never have married: (1) I was only 18. (2) We'd only known each other for a month before I got pregnant. (3) We knew very little about each other. (4) We both used drugs. We did agree to attend marriage counseling but found out later that it didn't help. James and I stayed together for several years, had our son Matthew, and the verbal and drug abuse was a consistent staple in our marriage. Though chaotic, I was able to finish school and receive my bachelor's degree in Fine Arts with a minor in Elementary Education. Our children witnessed a lot. I tried to stick it out for the kids but couldn't do it any longer. I left and moved right in with another man, Kris.

He was the ex-husband of a girl named Lylah who I met through a mutual acquaintance and made me a lot of money. Kris had been our drug supplier for me with Pot and James with Cocaine. We all became very good friends and once I left James, and a year after our divorce, Kris and I became a couple. I guess you could say we had a happy life. I was in love, I had my children and was living with a drug dealer who supplied me as well. Our relationship ended after I came back from drug treatment. My mother threatened that she wouldn't help me if I stayed with him. I listened but, six months later, after Kris was released from jail, we got back together. I desired to have a functional family. I proposed to him, and he turned me down because he found a new drug instead. I was pissed, but I moved on. (Today, Kris is in his last year of law school and plans to be a criminal defense attorney to help the innocent.)

Tyler would be my 1st introduction to the concept of 'sugar daddy' financier. He was a smart Insurance Broker and a seedy porn addict. We met at a concert where he was interested in having sex with my friend. She wasn't interested, but I had just learned how I could make some quick money by using what was between my legs. I offered, he accepted and kept accepting for eight months. At this point, I was addicted to money and was willing to put up with anything to receive it. There were times when our escapades were a little violent. Tyler thought he was in love with me, but I think he was more in love with the way I made him feel. Our escapades ended when he was sold meth instead of cocaine and went nuts from the high. He went into treatment. (Today, Tyler is now happily married to a swinger I once met.)

Jean, the attorney, would be my 2nd 'sugar daddy' financier. I met him when I was looking to file for divorce from James. His office was located on top of a bar I would frequent. Money had become my drugs of choice, and sex with his hands around my throat was the price I paid I did what I had to do to make my kids' lives easier and more fun, even if it meant risking my self-worth. Because of Jean, I could afford dinners out and vacations for my children. Our distant relationship of convenience would last for five years.

Then there was Mason. He was a drug dealer, an ex-convict and after two weeks of meeting him, we got married. I filed for divorce three weeks into the marriage because he spit in my face. During our whole time of knowing each other, he would give me drugs to keep me inebriated and under his control. Today, I'm not sure where he is, but I can guess he is probably is in jail.

Richard, I was sure would be the love that would last a lifetime. We met through my friend Jennifer on Thanksgiving Day. Let's say our love was passionate and instant, but within two months of us being together, I learned he abused drugs. However, his problems weren't going to deter my commitment to him, so I sprang into action of trying to save his life on a regular basis. He had this Jekyll and Hyde charm, sweet on one hand and hell on wheels when he used drugs. The physical abuse was the end of it for me when one day he threw my head against the nightstand my father gave me. As I tried to call 911, Richard threw me across the room and took the phone.

I ran to the bathroom to get away, and he shoved me up against the wall. I screamed, "Please stop!" and he listened. The next day I had a doctors' appointment to remove cancerous cells from my cervix. My doctor looked at my face and demanded I have an MRI. The test found I had a fractured cheekbone. He was later charged with simple battery.

After my relationship ended with Richard, I went to Biloxi Mississippi to meet up with my friend Chance. We hung out and used LSD. I thought it would be a great idea show up at Jean, the attorney's, door. His response, "Jillian, you left and met a guy who beat you. That was your choice!" I was pissed at his response and knew I really needed to get my life on track.

THE TURNING POINT

From the age of 14 through 25 having sex, violence and dysfunction in relationships were my normal and something I was comfortable with. My personal abuse of choice was Xananbar and Pot with the occasional dabbles in other things.

Of course, James was still in the picture because we had children together. One day, James called me on the telephone and shared that he had someone who wanted to score from me. James knew I had easy access to prescription drugs because of my street connections and relationships. I was reluctant to meet the person because I didn't know them, but he insisted. My mind was on leaving the next day to go and see my best friend in Tennessee. She paid for a flight for me to visit her and I was so excited. On the other hand, my addiction to money was always in play. After a lot of back and forth, we agreed that his friend would pick up the drugs at an area bank where my friend worked. James was adamant about me meeting his friend in person to the point of having the person call me himself saying he wanted Lortab. I explained what he needed to do and how to drop the money off, but the guy didn't feel comfortable transacting in that way. I told him I had to go and pick up my children and the only way I would wait is if he paid me extra and he agreed. Also, on this day was I really high off Xananbar and not totally on my alert game.

'The score' wanted to change the location and I agreed. We decided to meet at an area coffee shop. I walked inside with my hat and juicy couture sweats on and realized I didn't know anyone there. I left immediately, and as I am walking back to my car, this guy kept yelling my name. At first, I ignored him, but he caught up to me and said,

"You have my stuff?"

I replied, "I don't know what you are talking about" and kept walking.

He continued to follow me and then I turned around and say, "I know you are an f#$%&g cop!" and kept walking. He asked me what was in my hand and if I had his 'insurance papers' and I told him no. As I walked back to the car, I was handcuffed, and guns were shoved on both sides of my ribs telling me to get in the car. My friend is in the passenger seat holding the drugs in her purse, and they pull her out my car to arrest the two of us.

Yes, my ex-husband James, father of my two children, set me up to be arrested by an undercover narcotics cop to disrupt my life without him. Of course, I never made it to see my friend, stayed in jail for eight days and was sentenced to attend a drug treatment program.

The same year I was arrested for theft and later in 2011 a DWI. I remember the penal codes like it was yesterday. One count of R.S.14:67 Theft. One count of R.S. 40:969 Possession with intent to distribute Schedule IV (Xanax) R.S. 40:968 Possession with intent to disturb scheduled III (hydrocodone); R.S. 40:1041(D) Monies Derived from a drug transaction.

I can honestly say that I could not discern right or wrong because I was just living. I was accustomed to what I taught and caught from hanging with the wrong crowd. I made a conscious decision to pull myself up and work toward being a better person and doing the right thing. My journey to healing was starting.

I Learned

My mother was done with me. Remember, I had years of bad choices, several types of abuse, addictions, seven fiancés, and years of being the family embarrassment. I was very familiar with how to charm, take advantage, manipulate and get what I wanted despite what I had to endure to get it.

My dad passed away twenty years after his heart attack, and although I acted up a lot, he never gave up on me. I can't say what day it happened exactly, but 'it' finally hit me. What is 'it'?

- I am a child of God!
- I am beautiful!
- I am smart!
- I deserve the best!
- I deserve healthy love!
- My children deserve better!
- I don't need to use drugs!

I quickly learned, as soon as you make a conscious decision to make a change and do better, the best will come your way. I am a living witness to this and can say that I have all the above and more in my life.

HEALING BEGINS

It's a great thing to experience healthy love, and I believe it's what God intended for all of us. However, to grasp a hold of 'healthy love,' we need to dig deep and understand where our distorted way of dealing or engaging in relationships comes from. We seek to learn, not for the purpose of blame but to acknowledge so we can heal.

Part of my journey was to begin to listen to the few positive people who were around me and their unwillingness to be manipulated. They called me out on my stuff whether I liked it or not. There were Sonya and Carla from the drug treatment program. They kindly let me know that I was a drug dealer/user and were no better than the people who attended my program. I'm not sure why I thought I was. They showed me that it wasn't okay to sell my body for money.

I realized that I was always living in survival mode for myself and to take care of my children. Again, I realized that I deserved better for myself and them. When I left James, my first husband, and father of my children, I didn't have a plan. I knew I had to get out. I couldn't let my kids continue to see their mother be abused by their father. I did not want them to become another statistic. But I didn't know how to escape. Being with this abusive man had taken so much out of me. At the time, I had gotten a college degree, but he had brainwashed me and diminished my entire spirit and being. He told me I would never find anyone else, and I believed him. I bought into his judgment of me. I literally thought no one would want me because I was a woman with two children. It became so awful that I would look at myself in the mirror and be disgusted. I felt like I didn't know my own self. I would ask myself, who is Jillian

Edwards? I was constantly dosing myself with Xanax, Valium—whatever I could take in order not to feel. I had mastered the way to mask the pain of feeling. I felt so lost, in so many ways. My father had just died, and I had lost everything. I was scared. I had no one to help me. Even after leaving him, you read that I made more mistakes. However, I pushed forward and began my process of healing myself. Of course, this is the time when I finally met someone.

LONNIE

God knows just what you need, and he sent me an angel in the form of Lonnie. He came around during my time of soul searching and being by myself. No relationships, no men, no drugs, nothing! Our meeting was a little different from most men because he actually wanted to know and take care of me. I was closed off with a wall and electrified fence around me. He totally understood and took his time climbing over the walls and fences.

Lonnie consistently expressed his seriousness of getting to know me, the real Jillian, who deep down had a good heart and a strong desire to have a normal life, with a normal family, like the life I talked about having as a child. He was different because he didn't want anything but to be loved like I desired, to have a family like I desired and a spouse that would be there for him. After all, I had been through of kissing a lot of frogs; my king was found in Lonnie. He was the first and only person in my life to make me feel safe, confident, and my integrity was never on the line. He made me see the amazing person I was.

We had similar backgrounds of being brought up having faith in God. However, he was Baptist. No problem, he further professed his love for me by getting re-baptized and made all his sacraments in the Catholic Church. On March 13, 2013, we were married, and I haven't looked back. We did not have any children together and decided we would get pregnant with our love child Lonnie Coburn, IV who is growing up to be the kindest, lovingness, godly, and spirited child you will ever meet. His heart is holy and made from gold. We are six years in and my heart is happy because we both have what we wanted, and our family is filled with love. As I said, God knows what you need.

While I remain in this good space, I wonder how many women are out there in relationships of dysfunction and abuse. How many women want to make a change but not sure how? If that is you or someone you know, keep reading, and I will share exactly how I did it. Understand that just like me; you are beautiful, deserve the best of what God has for you and can position yourself for healthy love.

Daddy -

Robert 'Bob' Mark Edwards

There is a saying that girls learn how to be treated by men from the treatment of their father. Her decisions, who she dates and possibly marries, will be a result of her father was to her.

I absolutely adore my father. He stood 5'10, medium build with brown hair and piercing green eyes. Growing up he had a speech problem as well as several learning disabilities, but he overcame them to obtain several college degrees in Liberal Arts and Environmental Science from the University of Louisiana, Lafayette. He was the type of gentleman a southern belle desired. You know, the very polite man who will hold the door or stand up when a woman goes to walk away from a table. My mother was very blessed to have a man like him in her life. In his own way, he gave me hints early on of how a woman should be treated, but it would take me a long time to learn the lessons.

As told earlier in my story, he had a heart attack when I was five years old. After that, he struggled with his health for many years. I had a hard time leaving him home while I went out because I was afraid he would die without me being there. I'm not sure why I thought that, but I guess I was traumatized from his attack. My mom and dad switched roles, and he became the caretaker of the house with cooking, cleaning, and ironing. The house was spotless when my mother came home from work. He would sit under an old oak tree waiting for my sisters and me to come home from school. During the summers he would take us to our grandma's house and hung out on the family farm while he tended to the cattle.

As I grew up, I was told that I was supposed to be his son. It's funny how he tried to push me to be sportier and tom-boyish. I even played softball for a bit. I loved the smell of his old spice cologne and his hairy arms that held me for safe keeping. I am and will always be a daddy's girl.

Daddy was sad, depressed and often cried about how his life had changed. However, he tried to do his best in taking care of us and making sure we did what was right. Well, really tried to make sure I did the right thing. The going statement in our house was "What did Gigi do today?" He tried to protect me, keep me out of trouble, and control my every move if possible, to stop me from getting into trouble. Occasional spankings, punishments, but nothing worked. I would laugh at him when he yelled at me and would say he looked like 'The Hulk' from television with his green eyes. And if he called me Jillian, I was in serious trouble.

The older I got, the more protective he became. I had to call him when I went to my friends' house to prove I was there. I remember when I was 15, I went over to my friend's house to spend the night and we snuck out to meet some older boys. It was like my father had 'Spider-Man' senses because he knew we snuck out. Not only did he know, but he also found us at the place we snuck to. He yelled, once again, looking like the incredible 'Hulk' for me to get home. I was on punishment but ran away to my sisters' house because I didn't want to go home. Another time I let a guy drive my car and my father came from nowhere and screamed for everyone to get out of the car. He yanked me out and told me to go home. Before I could tell him I was pregnant with my daughter, he asked me, "Gigi, you're not pregnant, are you?"

On the one hand, he was always mad or disappointed because of how I behaved, but on the other, he would sometimes enable my behavior. For example, he would purchase booze for me because he didn't want me to get caught buying it or asking anyone else to do it. When I became pregnant with my first child, he was furious but helped me throughout my pregnancy, so I could finish school. He went to get my assignments, so I could do them at home. And when my daughter was born, he helped as much as he could by babysitting while I went to class.

My father knew all my stuff, got mad, yelled, but never gave up on me. He knew about my abuse with James. He knew that I was messing around with drugs and would pay my bills because my money went to selling and using. I could go on and on sharing story after story of how he cared for me. Not only was he there for me but I was there for him to hear what he loved, he feared, was deprived of, his sex life with my mother, his complaints, his hope, and dreams.

I was devastated when I learned he had Stage IV Hepatitis C. I will never forget the day he told me. I was outside their house playing with Gabby. He drove up with my mom, got out the car, picked up Gabby to hug her. He then put her down, began to cry and share that he had six months to live. My heart went into my stomach, and a piece of it was lost that day. He would always tell me how he wanted to see his granddaughter graduate from high school, college and see her get married. I hadn't shared with him that I was pregnant with my 2nd child, Matthew.

I tried my best to spend time with him. I would tell him, "Daddy, you're not sick, and I will see you tomorrow." I would call him during the day while his shows were on and he would tell me to stop bothering him, so he could watch his show. I was earnestly praying he would receive a miracle from God and be healed. I wanted to make sure I spoke to him every single day because I didn't know when would be the last time I would speak to him.

Sadly, my dad passed away on February 15, 2006. As I was being dropped to his house, he was being put in an ambulance. However, he was already gone.

Although I love my father, through prayer, therapy, and some intense conversations, I realized something. The relationship between my dad and I was not only inappropriate but enabling and dysfunctional. Let me be clear that I am in no way blaming my father for my choices. However, I am saying his treatment of me manifested in my choice of men. Yes, he loved me but always tried his best to control me and in every encounter.

There were incidents where he would scream at the top of his lungs in my face. I'd become used to it and at some point, thought it was funny. I was no longer scared of him. And, every guy I was in a relationship with was that 'Hulk' side of my dad in one way or another but with the touches of a southern gentleman. Interesting, huh?

THE HEALING CONTINUES

Once this epiphany happened, I could really do the work required to get my life back on track. Can you see a little bit of yourself or someone you know within my story? Are you questioning what to do at this very moment?

There were some pertinent details I had to understand and study for me to get where I am today. The rest of this book is designed to provide tips, information, and exercises on how you or a loved one can get back on track and live a life that is deserved and intended by God. This book is a guide to action and planning, but it is also a roadmap of positivity, love, and hope. If no one has ever told you that you can do it—that you can get out, and go on to live an amazing life, too! Guess what? I am telling you can!

OUR PATH TO HEALING

Perhaps my story is very familiar to you because it sounds like yours. Or, maybe it's the story of someone you love and want to help them live a better, productive life that they and God can be proud of. Whatever the case, there is a path to healing. The reason why I entitled this chapter 'Our Path' is because we are in this together. I cannot say that I am totally healed because healing is a daily process of work. Here are a few steps that I know will yield results. Keep reading and let's do this together.

STEP ONE

UNDERSTAND WHAT A "NORMAL" RELATIONSHIP LOOKS LIKE!

I honestly thought abuse was OK.

In fact, it took me years to learn it was wrong! After that first encounter with abuse, I went on to live through several abusive relationships. I was caught in the trauma and the drama. For a long time, I thought abuse—the hurt, the manipulation, the mental and physical abuse, and emotional anguish—was part of a "normal" relationship. I was suffering and hurting inside. It felt like there was no way out. Finally, I escaped. But it was a long journey. There were a lot of things I wish I would have known for an easier way to leave. Because I lived through it, I can teach you how to do it the easier way.

Freeing myself from abuse took a long time. Some of the things that made leaving harder were:

- Other people (including family) telling me the abuse was OK.

- Being afraid of the unknown and not wanting to be alone.

- Not wanting to reach out to others for help and feeling embarrassed about the abuse.

- Not believing I deserved better.

- Not knowing how to take care of myself physically, emotionally and loving myself.

- Not forgiving myself for my mistakes.

- Using drugs to mask my feelings, and not knowing how to deal with my emotions.

- Not having a plan. I believe God chose me because He knew I could withstand being uncomfortable and talking about things that, for most women who have been abused, trigger terrible moments. I'm not afraid to speak openly. I hope that doing so will help you.

Know that You Are Phenomenal!

I know the reason my three children are amazing is because I always remind them how great they are. You must remind those little ones how phenomenal they are. I'm here to remind you how phenomenal you are!

Picking up this book said your heart and mind were open to God's voice or a voice inside you that wants something better for yourself. YOU made it happen.

God chooses the ones who can handle it. He has seen you, now, He will guide you. Trust this truth: Now is your time. This IS your purpose. Your purpose will be a legacy one day, for your family, those you love and all who have helped you on your journey.

Self-Talk Exercise

Look at yourself in the mirror if you want, or just stand up and say out loud: "I am phenomenal!"

God does not make trash. He creates amazing things—and that is exactly what you are.

Remember one important thing: You are not the problem!

You did not ask to be scared if he is going to hit you again or yell at you, daily…

You did not ask to be on edge, daily…

You did not ask for any of it…

And none of it is your fault!

Repeat after me: "I did the best I could then; I am doing the best I can now!"

"Consult not your fears but your hopes and your dreams. Think not about your frustrations, but about your unfulfilled potential. Concern yourself not with what you tried and failed in, but with what it is still possible for you to do."

– Pope John XXIII

Your Thoughts

....
....
....
....
....
....
....
....
....
....
....
....
....
....
....
....
....
....
....
....
....
....
....
....

STEP TWO
RECOGNIZE WHAT ABUSE IS!

The Abuse "Cycle"

Most books, articles or resources on domestic violence talk about the "abuse cycle." This is a list of the stages of abuse. It gives a big picture view of how abuse develops.

It's important to remember that even though it's called an "abuse cycle," abuse isn't something you can predict. There's no way of knowing when things will suddenly get better—or worse. You won't be able to guess what he's going to do. He might even switch to another kind of abuse.

Stages of the "abuse cycle" are:

Tension Building

During this stage, the abuser is getting angrier and angrier. As he gets more and more upset, it becomes harder to talk to him and communicate with him. He doesn't listen to reason. At this stage, you might feel like it's your job to try and calm him down. It might feel like you must constantly "walk on eggshells" not to make him more upset.

Explosion

At this stage, the abuse occurs. The abuse can take many forms. It can be verbal, physical, sexual or emotional.

Apology or "Calm" Stage

After the abuse, there is a period when things seem calm. At this stage, he might apologize and say, "I'm sorry."

He may try to make it up to you by being nice to you or even buying you things. He might swear he'll never do it again. It's also possible that he will act like nothing happened or deny that anything happened and say that you're dramatic and overreacting.

This "nice stage" is all part of the abuse! The abuser is a master manipulator. He is the wolf hiding in sheep's clothing. Nice at first then, he wants to crush you! Make no mistake: Abusive men are the biggest manipulators. Everything they do is calculated. It is all part of the abuse. **Note:** Often, the longer a relationship goes on, the more likely it is that the "nice," "calm" and "making it up to you" stage will disappear completely. Leave before things get worse!

Real-Life Warning Signs

In real life, the "abuse cycle" shows up in all kinds of different ways. This is a list of things he might be doing that are signs of abuse. These are the warning signs that you are with a man who is dragging you down with an abusive relationship.

Warning 1 – He calls you back-to-back while you're at work, knowing you're working.

Warning 2 – He turns off his location service on his phone and doesn't come home.

Warning 3 – He tells you your happiness is too much and that you should stop hanging out with your girlfriends.

Warning 4 – He's negative about your family or the quality time you spend with them.

Warning 5 – He thinks he is inferior to your friends.

Warning 6 – He reminds you that he gave everything up for you.

Warning 7 – He tells you not to go to the gym or to skip an all girls' sport (this is him isolating you from the world).

Warning 8 – You look around and realize he has diminished everyone around you and suddenly it's just the two of you!

Warning 9 – He is constantly verbally and mentally abusing you! Examples: "I pay all the bills, what do you do?" or "I gave up my children for you! What are you doing for us?"

Warning 10 – When you are at the point of disgust with the person you are supposed to love, and he forces you to have sex with him.

Warning 11 – You're in debt, and you haven't a clue where the money is going. (Guess what? It's going to drugs or another woman.).

Warning 12 – You leave with your children to visit a friend out of town, and he is constantly checking in on you.

Warning 13 – He yells and screams and gets in your face.

Warning 14 – When you ask a question, he goes crazy and can't communicate with you.

Warning 15 – He controls all the money.

Warning 16 – He abuses alcohol or drugs on a regular basis.

Note: Abusers are threatened by anything you might do that could lessen your focus on him or your affection for him. For example, he might hate that you get a promotion at work or discourage you from having a hobby that brings you joy. He might even isolate you from your family and friends and the people who make you happy!

The Many Kinds of Abuse

There are many kinds of abuse. It's not always physical. He can be emotionally abusive to you, too. Abuse is all about power. He'll repeat a pattern of behavior to get--and keep--control over you, in as many ways as he can think of. Here is a list of the many kinds of abuse. You may have experienced all or some of them. Although I spoke about them earlier in the book, reiteration for better understanding is necessary.

Verbal Abuse

- Putting you down and/or calling you names
- Saying nasty things about you in public to make you feel ashamed in front of others
- Yelling and/or swearing at you
- Flying into rages
- Making your accomplishments sound small and meaningless
- Saying cruel and hurtful things
- Accusing you of things out of nowhere

Emotional Abuse

- Ignoring you
- Controlling your money or job
- Isolating you from others
- Being critical
- Threatening to hurt, kill himself, or you
- Threatening to take the kids away, if you have children

- Being suspicious of you and not trusting you
- Stalking or following you
- Saying what he's doing is no big deal when you bring it up or denying he's done any of it
- Reacting to you when you want to talk about it by exploding at you

Physical and Sexual Abuse

- Choking or strangling you
- Throwing or breaking things
- Holding you down or pressing you against the wall
- Pushing, slapping, shoving, punching, biting or kicking
- Using a weapon
- Forcing you to have sex (rape) or making you do things you don't want to do in bed, either with him or other people
- Using weapons during sex or hurting you

Be Kind to Yourself

I know it isn't easy to read lists like these. Some of these words might cause terrible memories. You might be feeling sad, hopeless, angry, scared or anxious. These emotions are all normal. Let's stop so you can take a moment to be kind to yourself!

Self-Guided Visualization Exercise

1. Close your eyes and imagine you are holding yourself gently.

2. As you embrace yourself, tell yourself, "It's going to be OK."

3. If you are crying as you do this, that's alright.

4. When you are ready to calm down, take a deep breath in. As you inhale, fill your lungs up with as much air as you can, all the way down to your belly area. You should feel your stomach inflate. Studies show that when you breathe this way, you automatically send a signal to your body to calm down. It helps to let go of stress, anytime. (You can do this whenever you need to. As you practice it more, try going slower and breathing in for 2-4 seconds, then letting a breath out for 2-4 seconds.)

5. Feel how strong you are! Be proud of yourself. You are here, reading this book because you are ready to move out of this mess. That is amazing!

"Love is patient, love is kind. It does not envy, it does not boast, it is not proud. It does not dishonor others, it is not self-seeking, it is not easily angered, it keeps no record of wrongs. Love does not delight in evil but rejoices with the truth. It always protects, always trusts, always hopes, always perseveres."

– 1 Corinthians 13:4-13

Your Thoughts

....
....
....
....
....
....
....
....
....
....
....
....
....
....
....
....
....
....
....
....
....
....
....
....
....

STEP THREE
LEARN TO LOVE YOURSELF

Tools for Loving Yourself

Don't wait for someone else to come along and tell you how great you are. Start telling yourself!

The tools below will help you grow to love for yourself and teach you how to respect and value yourself. I use them to help me get through the day when things get hard. I can always count on them to make me feel better. These tools will also give you the strength you need to rely on as you get ready to leave. They will help you build courage.

The Power of Positive Self-Talk

Positive self-talk is simple, but powerful. Sometimes, my positive self-talk will be as simple as saying to myself: "Jillian, you are awesome!"

I admit, when I first started, I thought it was sort of stupid. But then I gave it a try and the more I did it, the more I noticed a difference. For one thing, positive self-talk helped me feel better. It lifted my spirit. It made me feel energized. It also helped me identify better choices and make changes that improved my life. It propelled me out of hurtful relationships and into something better.

Positive self-talk will become one of the greatest "tools in your life box." It helps re-train your mind to be positive and reminds you to be kind to yourself. It gives you energy and builds confidence. For so long, a man has been abusing you with words. It's draining to hear an abuser say bad things to you. Hear yourself saying nice things about you! Practicing positive self-talk lets, you use your own words to fight back and remind yourself what's true: that you are amazing!

I still use positive self-talk today. It takes practice at first, and you need to keep doing it daily, but it's worth it. If you really do it, it works; trust me.

If I can do it, anyone can!

Always be careful what you say to yourself! Just because he's saying mean things to you doesn't mean you have to repeat them to yourself. Remember: You want to say positive things to yourself about who you are.

Self-Love Exercise

Each morning start by saying one to three nice things about yourself. If you're worried, you'll forget them, write them down and read them out loud.

If you're having trouble coming up with them, here are some ideas:

I am strong

I am smart

I am beautiful

You can repeat these thoughts anytime you need to during the day, but the one thing you must do is repeat them again, word for word before you go to bed at night. This way, you begin and end your day by hearing loving, positive words.

Your Thoughts

....
....
....
....
....
....
....
....
....
....
....
....
....
....
....
....
....
....
....
....
....
....
....
....
....

Don't Fall for the Negative Voices

Random, mean thoughts can show up in your head to try and trick you. They can say all kinds of negative things, including that you're not good enough, smart enough, or pretty enough. They can say, "You'll never be with anyone better." Don't listen to the horrible things these voices are saying to you! When they show up, recognize them for what they are, lies. Instead, replace the sound of those voices with positive statements.

Quick Tip

There's another simple thing I learned about in treatment that I used to protect my self-esteem. It's an easy way to stop receiving the hateful things a man would say to me.

All I did was put down the phone when he (my ex) would belittle me. This made it easier not to absorb the negative things he was saying. After all, they weren't true!

Mantras and Affirmations

Other exercises that I use to improve my self-esteem and strengthen my love for myself are mantras and affirmations.

Mantras and affirmations are like positive self-talk, only more focused. They help you stay clear about what you want for yourself and your life. When you get into the habit of using them, they can help you think positively on a regular basis, boost your confidence and reduce stress and anxiety.

MANTRAS

A mantra is a meaningful word that you repeat to yourself, silently or out loud, to help focus your thoughts. Mantras calm your body and your mind. Use a mantra when you feel like your thoughts are scattered or confused, or when you want to remind yourself to focus on what's important.

Some examples of mantras are:

- Love
- Hope
- Peace
- Om (this is an ancient word linked to the divine, pronounced "Ohhhm." You don't have to be religious to use this word; it is easy to chant and makes a humming sound that is calming.)

Mantra Exercise

Choose your mantra from the list above or think of a word that is meaningful to you.

Sit on the floor with your legs crossed.

Close your eyes and slow your breathing.

Say your mantra either out loud, quietly or silently if you are more comfortable.

Repeat your mantra as many times as you need to feel calm and focused.

Your Thoughts

....
....
....
....
....
....
....
....
....
....
....
....
....
....
....
....
....
....
....
....
....
....
....
....
....
....
....

AFFIRMATIONS

Like a mantra, affirmations can be spoken out loud or silently in your head.

Affirmations are a little longer than mantras. An affirmation is a very personal statement about your goals and what you want. An affirmation helps you remember and focus on what you want to achieve in life, who you want to be or somewhere you want to go. When you use an affirmation, you help yourself work on making that goal happen, right now, just by thinking about it.

Like positive self-talk, affirmations can be powerful. In fact, it was a scientist in the 1970s who developed the practice of saying affirmations to help rewire negative thought patterns. Affirmations literally help reshape your brain! Some examples of affirmations are:

- I am lovable and worthy of love.

- I am powerful!

- I can create change.

- I am courageous.

- I trust me to take care of me--always!

Affirmation Exercise

Get a pen, pencil or markers and some paper.

Choose one or several affirmations from the list above and write them down. Or, write your own affirmation:

1. Begin by writing for 5-10 minutes, reflecting on what you want for yourself in life. Write down anything you want, no matter how impossible it seems.

2. Look at your list and choose 1-3 things to focus on.

3. Fill in the sentence with your goal:

"I can [insert what you want to do here], and I will [insert what you want to do here]."

Your Thoughts

....
....
....
....
....
....
....
....
....
....
....
....
....
....
....
....
....
....
....
....
....
....
....
....
....

Repeat your affirmations loud or in your head to start and finish your day, and during the day if you want to. Each time you say your affirmation, really feel how much you believe in this affirmation, in every part of your body.

Use affirmations, mantras, and positive self-talk as much as needed. Feel free to choose whichever works best for you. They are all valuable "tools in your life box" that will have a positive effect on how you think of yourself, strengthen your self-esteem and help you accomplish things that you used to think were too hard.

Self-Forgiveness

Forgiving yourself is an important step to rebuilding your self-esteem and learning to love yourself. When you tell yourself "I forgive you," you accept all of you, including the mistakes you may have made. Accepting yourself allows you to become whole.

Once I forgave myself and accepted myself, I really started to like the woman I am! This is a powerful feeling. Forgiving myself and accepting myself means choosing me, now and forever.

Guided Visualization Exercise

Think about something you feel like you did wrong or a mistake you wish you hadn't made.

It's OK to feel regret and sadness. Remember, you did the best you could at the time. You're still doing your best now.

Say to yourself: "I forgive you!"

Take a moment to feel lightness in your body as you think, "I forgive me." This lightness is the feeling of the weight of guilt and shame that you had been carrying for so long, being lifted off your shoulders.

Your Thoughts

....
....
....
....
....
....
....
....
....
....
....
....
....
....
....
....
....
....
....
....
....
....
....
....
....

Let Go of the Past, Welcome the Future

By telling myself, I forgive myself and saying: "Jillian, you did your best," and really knowing that it's true, I learn to let go of the past, and open new possibilities for the future.

Forgiving myself means I am kind to myself. Practicing this inner kindness allows everything in my world around me—including plants, air, people, animals—know that I am an infinite being who is open to something better in her life.

Learn to forgive yourself, every day! It is the greatest kindness. It helps you let go of the past and open the door so that something amazing can show up.

STEP FOUR
EVALUATE YOUR BEHAVIOR

When you're in an abusive relationship, you do not want to feel. Who wants to reflect on something he did that dug a knife into your heart? "Not me!" I used to say!

Often, we are completely blocked. We do not want to deal with our emotions and what is causing them. Facing our feelings and facing reality just seems too hard. Sometimes, we make things worse by doing drugs to numb ourselves and block any feelings that might cause us pain. This happened to me!

I was thirteen when I began smoking weed and drinking every weekend—that's 27 years of putting drugs and alcohol in my body! Any doctor, therapist or health professional will tell you I limited my brain's capabilities by choosing alcohol and drugs to control my life.

Using Drugs, Hurting Others

I couldn't find solutions when I was intoxicated and on drugs. I also didn't see how much I was hurting the people around me.

When you are abusing drugs, do you think you are aware of the pain you are causing others? Nope. Why? Because you are so caught up in masking the pain.

I couldn't resist the drugs. Not even thinking about my nine-year-old daughter and four-year-old son could stop me — my poor little babies. I didn't stop to think about what I was doing to them until I was arrested.

It's was hard to face that I messed up my kids for a while, ruined my reputation and almost lost my license to teach because I decided selling drugs was more important.

Today, I know that my soul and my kids are more important than the next high.

Warning: if you're going to abuse drugs, be willing to take the awful things that will come your way! Drugs will ruin your reputation and make your life worse. If you're arrested, a track record with drugs will make it harder to get a job. After I was arrested, I lived with my mom for two years. During that time, I couldn't teach because of the drug charges, and the only job I could get was one where they wouldn't run a background check.

Drugs limit your choices, they limit your future, and they restrict how awesome your life can be!

Warning Signs You're Using Too Much

Here are some important signs and symptoms you are using too much:

- You get prescription drugs from a drug dealer.
- You make sure it's 12:00 pm (Like the song Jimmy Buffet) somewhere and drink close to two bottles of wine just to fall asleep.
- You are sick at least once a month.
- You look at your bank account and make sure that you have enough money to buy your stash.
- You start counting your prescription pills, making sure you have enough to last you.
- You sell your own prescriptions to buy other prescription drugs on the street.
- The chemicals you are putting in your body make you angry and unaware.

- You wake up and don't know the person who is sleeping next to you.

We have one soul. Our soul chose the body we are in. Why would we put waste into these beautiful bodies?

From Hurting Myself to Finding the Real Me

It took going to jail and being drug-free for two years to find the true Jillian: the person--the mind, spirit, and body--who needed to love herself. When I was on drugs, I couldn't see how important it was to love me. The real, true me needs to be loved and not fed with poison and drugs!

You can find the real you, too. Don't wait until you're arrested or in some other kind of trouble to make a change! Don't waste years of your life in the darkness of drugs. Stop poisoning yourself and start learning to love yourself.

Self-Talk Exercise

"I refuse to damn myself by giving my life to the drug and alcoholic world that is all around us."

"I refuse to be the next statistic." "I choose to take care of my body instead."

Your Thoughts

....
....
....
....
....
....
....
....
....
....
....
....
....
....
....
....
....
....
....
....
....
....
....
....
....

There's Another Way

Do you think I asked my body if it desired four bars (Xananbar) a day? No, I just did what I thought I had to do to wake up in the morning and face my life—and continue to mask the pain of sadness, grief, depression, anger and despair I felt for my life. (How heavy is that statement? It's pretty heavy for me to write).

But there is another way. I didn't have to run from my feelings by numbing myself. Instead, I could have faced my feelings and learned how to deal with them. Learning how to manage my emotions could have helped me get out of a bad relationship faster—and into a rewarding life, I love, like the one I have now, a lot sooner.

Why Facing Feelings Is Important

Back then, I didn't really understand what feelings or emotions were. I knew they made me cry, laugh, smile, and sometimes burst into anger. But that's it. I didn't know why I had them—or what to do with them.

Today, I understand more about how emotions work. I know I don't have to avoid them and that I can feel them, safely. Facing my feelings instead of shoving them down or running from them is an important part of taking care of myself.

Learning how to handle feelings is important for everyone, especially if you are in an abusive relationship. When you can't manage your feelings, they can take over your mind, and you risk staying when you should get out.

To put it another way, if you do not have the right tools to deal with your emotions, you will end up in the same position with the same problems!

Don't Run from Feelings

Being in touch with your feelings might sound scary. But it's worse to run from them. When we don't take the time to feel and instead bury our emotions inside, they can burst open out of nowhere--hurting ourselves and those around us. Or, we shove them down so deep that they constantly make us miserable.

The truth is that feelings aren't so scary if you know how to face them. Taking the time to know what you're feeling, and experience it, means you can let your feelings go.

In this way, you experience emotions--while also being separate from them and not having them run your life. You are still "at one" with them—they are still a part of what makes you, you—but they don't control you or define you.

For example, if you are sad, you can feel sad, and grieve or cry if you need to. But you can also let those feelings go once you've experienced them and move on. You don't have to give in to sadness forever. Feel the feeling then, let the feeling go. In this way, you can move on.

Remember:

- You are not your feelings.
- You do not have to act on your feelings unless you want to. You decide what to do about how you feel.
- You can have a feeling then let it go and move on.

Basic Feelings

Don't be afraid to have feelings. Your feelings just are. There are no "bad" feelings.

Remember, feelings are only a problem when you try and run from them or are so unaware you let them decide all your actions without thinking.

For example, if you're angry but don't take the time to recognize the feeling, you will probably just walk around all day feeling mad at the world--and yell at someone for no reason. That's letting your feelings decide your actions for you. Instead, if you take the time to say to yourself, "I'm angry," think about why that might be (it's OK if you don't always know the answer, it might show up later), and experience the feeling...then, you can let it go. The basic feelings are:

- Anger
- Joy
- Sorrow
- Surprise
- Fear
- Disgust
- Guilt or shame
- Interest

Each one of these has many different descriptions. For example, sorrow is also known as: "sadness, hurt, despair, depression, unhappiness, misery, suffering, hopelessness."

Evaluation Exercise: Figuring Out Your Feelings

1. Get a journal.

2. Next to the date, list some of the feelings you experienced that day. Remember, there are no negative or "bad" emotions.

3. Sit with those feelings, even if it's uncomfortable.

4. If having a feeling makes you remember something bad that happened, a time that someone hurt you, go to the feeling. Comfort yourself. Tell yourself you did the best you could!

5. Now, let go of those feelings.

6. Feel proud of yourself for having the courage to face your emotions.

7. Finally, try to let in a feeling of joy, love, and peace.

Your Thoughts

....
....
....
....
....
....
....
....
....
....
....
....
....
....
....
....
....
....
....
....
....
....
....
....

Preparing to Grieve the End of a Relationship

Feeling isn't always easy. But it is an important step to letting go and moving on. It's also an important tool for dealing with change including the biggest change of all: getting out of an abusive relationship and starting over to live the life you want.

One way to prepare to leave, and make sure you don't go back, is to prepare yourself for how you might feel.

When I left, I had to face feelings like sadness and anger. Even though I knew it was best to leave, I still had to grieve the end of the relationship. I had to take the time to feel sad, and angry, and all the things I was feeling. I couldn't run from those emotions.

Facing these feelings wasn't easy, but it was the right choice. If I hadn't, I would have ended up running from my feelings...running from the pain of my emotions... and running right back to him!

Take the time to feel your emotions. You are worth it. After all, instead of spending energy trying to get him back, you'll be spending energy on YOU!

Understanding Anger

Sometimes we think that anger is a "bad" feeling. It isn't. Anger is a natural defense that kicks in to protect us from people who are hurting us or crossing personal boundary. In other words, anger is the response to the unwanted action of another person. It can be set off by sadness, being frightened, feeling threatened or feeling lonely.

Women often cover up anger with sadness. This is because it's more acceptable in our society for women to be sad than angry.

The next time you feel sad or like crying, ask yourself: "Am sad or am I angry? It's OK to feel angry! It's important to know how to handle the feeling of anger. Otherwise, you risk turning your anger on other people--or yourself. You're the last person who deserves the pain of more anger! In knowing how to manage a feeling of anger in the right way, you will get the benefits of anger: motivation, energy, and empowerment.

Tell yourself: it's OK to be angry!

Your Feelings—Not His

One of the things abusers do is project their feelings into you. They make you feel like everything is your fault.

When a feeling occurs, ask yourself: Is it yours? Or is it his?

Are you really upset about the event that happened? Or is he upset?

When I have a feeling, I ask: Is this really mine or someone else's?

By checking in like this, I can identify the source.

If it's not my feeling, I simply say, "Oh great, not mine...bye!" I break the connection to another person's feeling. This keeps me from being stuck in shit that literally is not even mine!

STEP FIVE
MAKE A DECISION!

Many abused women will say they're going to leave, but they never do.

They "get stuck," staying for all sorts of reasons. They get stuck using drugs; they get stuck running away from their feelings, they get stuck not wanting to leave a life that they're used to.

In this Chapter, I'm going to tell you about some of the things that can get you stuck, so you can be prepared to conquer them.

Don't Let Shame Stop You

One of the most powerful things that can stand in the way of leaving is shame, the feeling, and belief that you are defective, that you are beyond repair.

When my first marriage turned abusive, I did not want to be judged by my family or the church. I felt like I didn't want to break the laws of the Catholic Church, where I was married. For me to get married again, I had to fill out a document detailing what happened to make me want to leave. I was afraid of being judged for being alone after I left, and I was afraid of being judged for being abused.

The next relationship I had was not marriage, but I was still scared to show my mom the bruises and pain the abuser inflicted on me. For years, I hid my physical and emotional pain so well! I did not want anyone to know.

Don't make the mistakes I made. You are not defective, and fear of change is normal, not something to shy away from. Reach out to people who can help you. Get a plan together. And get out!

Don't Stay to Be Taken Care Of

I have a friend who was in an abusive relationship. She did everything I told her to do, and she got out. But soon, she went back.

"I like my life the way I was," she told me. She missed how her husband took care of her.

I asked her, "You like the lifestyle, but do you like the abuse? Do you want to be abused because you said something wrong? Or do you want to be able to speak your mind and not live in fear all the time?"

When you've spent so much time in the mentality of a man taking care of you, it's hard to think about leaving and start a new life. It can feel like the rug is pulled out from under you. But there isn't any lifestyle that makes living with abuse "worth it!" Do not stay with someone who makes you afraid for your life!

Mary needed a support team of friends and family cheering her on to remind her why she had to leave and to remind her that she could do it. She finally got out for good!

Don't Believe Him When He Says He Will Change

If you are with an abuser or an addict, they never change. They will slip up again. If he did it once, guess what: It will happen again, and again and again.

If you are being abused, the person can't change, and you won't be able to change them.

Believe me, I have been abused by ten people in my lifetime, and I tried everything, hoping and praying on my rosary to change them.

Guess what? They never changed

But I did. I left!

Living through the same thing over and over, hoping it will change and only to see the same results again and again. It is craziness! The only way out is to leave.

Let me ask you: What are we afraid of losing? Someone who tears us down?

That is not why God created us. He didn't create us for someone to walk all over us and use us!

Don't Wait for Something or Someone to "Save You"

Growing up, I used to think there was a fairy godmother that lived in the back of our yard who, no matter what I did, could come in and fix everything for me. Guess what? That's wrong! That's not life.

You must make change happen for yourself.

Don't Listen to Other People When They Tell You the Abuse is OK

Don't listen when people say, "get over it; it's going to get better."

I still remember being eighteen, about to walk down the aisle to marry a man who had already abused me. My aunt knew about the abuse. I wasn't sure if I should marry a man who was hurting me. I asked her what to do.

She told me to go ahead and get married. She said, "Everything is worth fighting for."

Well, let me say this about that: Not abuse!

Don't listen when the people around you tell you the abuse is OK!

Don't Think You "Have to" be in Relationship

Don't let a voice inside your head tell you that you must be in a relationship to be a valuable and lovable person. Sometimes we make the mistake of assuming that we need a relationship to be whole. We think that if we aren't in a relationship, there's something "wrong" with us. (And that only if we are in a relationship, is there something "right" with us.) We start to think a bad relationship is superior to no relationship. It's not true! If you're in an abusive relationship, you should get out. You have a right to get out and live a life that isn't ruled by fear and suffering!

Don't Let Fear of the Unknown Stop You!

Fear of the unknown is a powerful thing. For a long time, I feared my own actions; I didn't want to think about the new life I would create by leaving the man I was with. It was terrifying to wonder about what it would be like to be alone. It's like swimming when we are young: we fear what the deep might hold.

You have the strength you don't even know you have! You can count on yourself.

Don't Believe It's Your Fault

Many abusers convince you that it's your fault. Abusive men are great manipulators! They never accept that they are wrong. They make you believe that you caused them to do things (well, if that were true, guess what? He could walk away if you were really the crazy one!) The truth is you're not the crazy one. He is!

The deeper truth is it's never just one person's fault in a relationship. It's his choice to abuse you, and it's your choice if you stay. In his mind, your continuing to be in the relationship communicates that his behavior is ok. If you leave and come back, he will go back to abusing you. He is addicted to abuse, and you are his drug of choice. You are not a person to him; you are a thing to manipulate and control.

Wake-Up Call: You Have to Make the Choice

How many people do you know who have shitty relationships but won't leave?

Are you reading this now and realizing that you are one of those people?

We have a choice in our lives. You can react to it and resist it, or you can acknowledge it and choose something else. Only you can make a choice to get out.

Repeat After Me: I can't change the person who is abusing me. The only person I can change is ME!

STEP SIX
CREATE A PLAN!

Abuse is the toughest thing to get out of. But you can do it! Having a plan makes it possible.

This Chapter will walk you through different parts of your plan and explain why they are important. I will share with you what worked for me, and what I wish I had known how to do. Then, you can put together a plan that works best for you. Your plan must fit your life and the situation you're in. A plan is a key to the door that unlocks a better future.

Why You Should Plan

Plan and be prepared! This makes it so much easier to leave.

Even if you're just thinking about leaving, make a plan- -now. It gives you something to fall back on if things get suddenly worse. You must protect yourself! And, if you have kids, you have to protect them.

Having a plan means you can get out, fast if you need to. Remember: You don't have to use your plan right away, but you should have one. Just in case plan your escape.

When the time comes, you'll be ready.

Be Safe

The most important thing when putting a plan togeth- er is to be safe.

For a lot of women, the most dangerous time is right after leaving. Think through all the risks ahead of time!

Think about where and when he might know where you will be if he tries to find you after you leave. If you're having trouble thinking all of it through and don't know how to prepare, reach out to someone who can help. This could be someone you can trust who knows you and your relationship or a professional.

Why You Need Support

As part of your plan, you will need help from other people. There's nothing to be ashamed of about reaching out to others. Everyone needs people to help them through the big things in life. You need people to help make your plan work, and you need people to support you through the emotional ups and downs.

As you prepare to leave or start thinking about leaving, you may start to have doubts or begin to back out. You may start to believe (incorrectly) that:

He'll change (he never will!)

You are the only person who can see the "good" in him (there isn't any "good" in an abuser!)

You can "fix" him (you can't!)

The support of friends and family can help you when you start to backslide. They can make sure you commit to your plan to leave. They can remind you of all the good that lies ahead and encourage you to be strong.

Accountability Friend

An accountability friend will help you stay focused on leaving. If you try and go back to him, they will help you stick to your commitment to leave. They can help you get prepared and help you after you leave.

"In Life, you will realize there is a role for everyone you meet. Some will test you, some will use you, some will love you, and some will teach you. But the ones who are truly important are the ones who bring out the best in you. They are the rare and amazing people who remind you why it's worth it."

— Unknown

Planning: Keep Track of the Abuse

One of the most powerful things you can do if you are thinking of leaving is starting a record of the abuse.

You will be so glad you did!

I cannot stress this enough to you guys: DOCUMENT ANY ABUSE: PHYSICAL OR MENTAL!

Here's how to do it:

- Keep evidence of the abuse, like pictures.
- Keep a journal of each episode of abuse, if it's safe for you to do so. For each entry, write down: Date, what he did, what threats he made.

If the worst happens and you are injured, go to the hospital or ER. Tell them to document your visit. This is gathering evidence!

Remember: Work on your plan to get out! The longer you stay, the worse it gets.

Planning: The PPO and Other Paperwork

You'll want to gather as much paperwork ahead of time as you can. You'll also need to be prepared to get a PPO and make copies of it.

How a PPO (Police Protection Order) Works

The first thing you will do after you get a PPO from the court is make several copies of it, along with copies of the abuser's photo.

Here's why: you want to make sure you always have one copy on you and give one copy each to the police; your boss; along with his picture.

If you have children, give one to teachers at their schools and all the people who care for them, including babysitters.

Collect as many important documents ahead of time as you can. You will need them after you leave.

Documents

Driver's license

Passports, birth certificates, marriage certificates, and bank statements, social security cards school and medical records driver's license, car registration

Change passwords online, including: bank accounts, phone, email, other resources you use such as credit cards and Welfare Identification

Planning: Protecting Your Home

Think ahead to what might happen after you leave. Be prepared to protect your home if he will be leaving or know how to be safe in your new location if you will be moving. Thinking ahead will help keep your personal things, your home, your bank account, yourself and your kids safe.

At Home

If he has left your home:

- Change your phone number or make sure you have your own cell phone.

- If you have a landline phone, ask the phone company to request caller ID. Ask that your number always be blocked so that whenever you call someone, no one can see your new, unlisted number.
- Change the locks!
- Add outside lights to your home. If you can, install a security system such as a Motion Sensitive Lighting System.
- Consider putting in stronger doors. Steel or metal doors are much stronger than wood doors.
- Make sure you have smoke and carbon monoxide detectors and that they have fresh batteries. **Always keep spare batteries on hand in a place you know you will be able to find them.

If you are moving to a new home:

Consider renting a Post Office Box or borrowing a friend or neighbors address for your mail. Keep in mind: your address will be listed on restraining orders and police reports. Try to be careful who you give your new address to.

Tell Others

Whether or not you can afford your security system, use the eyes and ears of your neighbors to help! Tell them your abuser has left and ask them to please call the police if they see him near your home (or near your kids if you have children). Tell your friends the same thing.

- Make sure you have someone who can help you anytime you feel down! Have a friend or trusted family member "on call" who you can reach out to anytime you feel sad or upset.

- Find support groups or workshops in the area that you can drop into if you need to.
- Other Things to Do If You Have Kids
- Change the route to and from school.
- If possible, change your children's schools.

At Work

- Change your work hours and find a new way to get to and from work.
- Give your boss a copy of the PPO and a picture of the abuser.
- Tell a trusted coworker about what happened and ask them to screen your calls.
- Practice a safety plan for your workplace. Make sure it includes arriving and leaving and that it covers going in and out of the building and/or parking area near your workplace.

Everywhere Else

Don't go to the same stores or businesses that you did when you were with the abuser.

When you hang out with friends or go out to eat, choose new places.

Legal Battles: You Can Be Brave

If you end up facing a legal battle as I did, you will need to be brave. You can do it! Document everything and save it in a save all evidence in a safe place.

Your Life, Your Plan

- Your plan must fit your life and the situation you're in. You may have just left a man who hardly notices when you come and go, or he may be the type who tracks your every move and begin stalking you after you go. Your plan for leaving would be different in each situation.

  Think through what might happen based on the specifics of your own life and plan the right way. If you can't do it alone, reach out for help.

Practice Your Plan

- Be ready in case your children tell your partner about your plan or he finds out.

- Practice ways you could leave the house without being noticed. For example: walking a pet, going to the store, or taking out the trash. These are all opportunities you can use if needed to escape spur of the moment. Review your plan often.

- If you are not smart and you do not follow the plan, he may make things worse for you!

Key Parts of Your Plan

Think ahead to where you will go if you won't be staying in the home or moving to a new home. Try and think of four places you could go to if you must leave. Think through these other key pieces of your plan.

Shelter

Know where you can go. Find a shelter, church or another shelter, or talk to friends or family and ask if you can stay with them.

Money

- Set aside money for you to use as soon as you leave. Save some up if you can or buy vouchers. If you need to, prepay some expected bills, like your cell phone bill.

- Open a bank account in your name only.

- Plan on getting a job after you leave. Do all the important planning you need to do to help you get a job beforehand, such as updating a list of skills or your resume or making a list of people you know who might be hiring or know of work who you can contact after you leave.

What You Will Bring

If it's Safe, take these things with you:

- Children (if it is safe)

- Money

- Keys to car, house, and work (Hide an extra set of car keys)

- A bag of clothes for you and your children. If you don't think it's safe to hide this at home, ask a friend you can trust or a neighbor if you can leave it there. (Try not to leave the bag with friends that you both have, a neighbor that lives right next door, or family members.)

- Medicine and medication

- Heirlooms or objects that are special to you. Set them aside somewhere safe and pack them up when you can so they are ready to go with you.

Phone: Communication

Some shelters or centers might be able to give you a cell phone programmed to only call 911.

- Set aside important phone numbers: police, friends, hotlines, and the local shelter.
- Teach your kids how to use 911. Make up a code word you can use that will be the signal they need to make the call.
- Check in with a domestic violence hotline on a regular basis to talk to someone about your options and have someone to offer support.
- Know where the closest pay phone is in your neighborhood.
- Don't be afraid to call the police.

Fast Escape

If you think you may need to make a fast escape, always have gas in the car and park with the car facing the street. Practice leaving safely. Practice with your kids, too.

After you leave, if he shows up, call the police right away! They need to enforce the restraining order.

If You're Not Ready to Go Yet: Staying Safe

The number one thing you should do if you're with an abuser is leave. The longer you stay questions your level of safety. If you are still with your abuser and feel like you can't leave yet or need more time to plan, there are things you can do to be as safe as possible.

At Home

Identify the safest areas of the house. These are places where there are no weapons and where there are ways to escape (a door, a window). Try to go these areas if arguments start.

If you have children, don't run to them as he may hurt them as well.

If you can't escape violence, make yourself a small target by going into a corner and curling up into a ball. Protect your face and put your arms around each side of your head, with your fingers laced together protecting your head and face.

Keep weapons locked away, if you have them in the house. Try and think of ways to get them out of the house.

Make sure your kids know a safe place to go, like a room with a lock, or a friend or neighbor's house. Make sure they know their job is to stay safe no matter what.

STEP SEVEN
SEEK PEACE

Being abused is like being caged. When the cage is released, you have been so brainwashed to believe there is no way out...when all along there was this huge universe waiting for us.

How many of us have made it our purpose to help or take care of others, no matter what happens? Start choosing for YOU!

Just because you've experienced what you have doesn't mean you don't have a right to a great life just like everyone else. You can recreate what you have experienced and turn it into something magnificent: your own life. You are beautiful a child of God!

Stay Safe

Even though you have left him, you still need to take steps to stay safe. Be sure to follow the guidelines on pages in Step 6.

Developing a New Point of View

I know what it's like to feel confused. For so long I had listened to everyone else's point of view. I didn't even realize the capacity I had to do things. Over time, I slowly built the self-esteem and an awareness of how powerful I am.

As you move forward, stay safe, continue practice being nice to yourself, and be patient with yourself if things are challenging.

Peace Exercise

Try adding a gratitude exercise to your day. Each morning, be grateful for two things. Every time you see your reflection, say something amazing about yourself and tell yourself why you are grateful to be you.

Your Thoughts

....
....
....
....
....
....
....
....
....
....
....
....
....
....
....
....
....
....
....
....
....
....
....
....

Practice Being Kind to Your Mind and Body

- Keep practicing your positive self-talk, mantras, and affirmations. They are an important part of keeping your mind, spirit, and body healthy.

- Take good care of your body. Live these healthy habits, and you won't be tempted by drugs, alcohol or another abusive man:

- Exercise

- Seeing a therapist if you can, or a pastor or other spiritual guide

- Practice Yoga

- Walk outside and be in communion with nature

- Being kind to your body

- Prayer, if you are religious

Each day I ask myself, "What grand and glorious day will I create today?" I ask this question not to seek an answer but to remind myself to be open to whatever the day may bring. Try starting your day this way. See what possibilities you can imagine for yourself.

Brain Dump Exercise

Get some paper and a pen.

List all the things that are worrying or causing you anxiety.

After writing them down, go outside and say those things one at a time, either out loud quietly or in silence.

Then, tear up the paper.

Your Thoughts

....
....
....
....
....
....
....
....
....
....
....
....
....
....
....
....
....
....
....
....
....
....

You cannot move forward if you are still stuck on things in the past.

Move forward--the world is waiting for you to let go, and let God show you the way!

Getting to Know YOU

The exciting part about being in this new chapter is that you will have the chance to get to know someone new: you!

Be patient with yourself. As you begin your new life, you might find that making choices for yourself is sometimes hard. That's OK. You will slowly learn how to make the best decisions for you.

You won't know how to do it all right away. It's ok if you mess up. No one is perfect.

I am still forgiving and telling myself that day by day I am getting better. So, will you!

Please believe in yourself. Please get to know you. Please try to realize you are doing your best!

I finally found me. She is kind, funny, compassionate, enduring, smart, smiles a lot and isn't judgmental; she makes people happy and is a forward thinker, a lover, a hugger, and sober, creative, and aware!

You can find you, too.

Remember: The truth is, we are all infinite beings.

Reflective Exercise

It can be helpful to take time to think about what you believe about life. Do you have a positive outlook or a negative one? Often, that viewpoint isn't even ours—it belongs to our former abuser!

Take the time to think through what you believe.

Get a piece of paper and a pen.

List viewpoints and "truths" about life, like "Life is hard," "Nothing comes easy," etc.

Then, take a close look at those "truths" and "rules" to see if they really belong to you. Are they yours? Or do they belong to the man you used to be with?

You can create your own rules, now!

Your Thoughts

....
....
....
....
....
....
....
....
....
....
....
....
....
....
....
....
....
....
....
....
....
....
....
....

Imagining Better Things

The power of the mind is truly remarkable. Often, we do not realize we have the power to shift all this energy just by changing our thought patterns.

Instead of thinking about what you don't have, be willing to ask the universe for what you want! Be willing to see things show up that you never thought of or dreamed could happen.

Meditation Exercise

Every day for the past four years, I have a ritual to begin my day. I find a beautiful outdoor spot and meditate. I think about having everything contribute to me, and I contribute back to the earth.

Your Thoughts

....

....

....

....

....

....

....

....

....

....

....

....

....

....

....

....

....

....

....

....

....

....

....

It's easy! Leave any device in your car. Find a comfortable place to sit. Open your eyes and breathe in and out. Really look at what you see and what the world has to offer.

By doing this, you are showing the universe that you are willing to receive the abundant beauty of life.

Forgiving Others

Sometimes a lot of our energy gets taken up in hating someone who has wronged us.

In these cases, it can be worth it to practice forgiveness not because they deserve it, but because it sets us free.

When you're ready, you might feel like forgiving someone else might be helpful to you by freeing up energy or resentment.

Note that forgiveness doesn't mean you need to see or talk to anyone! It isn't about the other person; it is something you do for you. Forgiveness is about freeing yourself from any connection to that other person by letting go of any bitterness you have been holding on to.

For me, it took forgiving the ex and what he had done to me to move forward. I needed peace. I was destroying my life and everything that I wanted to create. That simple forgiveness set me free. This does not mean I forgot what had happened; it just means I moved forward and no longer sat in the flames, boiling and being angry.

Soft-hearted people are not fools. They know what people did to them, and they forgive anyway. This opens space in their hearts for something better to show up!

Healthier Relationships

As you live a new life, pay attention to who is around you, romantically and socially. Learn how to start new and healthy relationships, when you're ready.

Avoid the Drama

Look at the people you choose to spend time with. Are the people around you asking for ease, joy, and glory in life? Or do they get caught up in the drama that makes them suffer? Do they always seem to make things difficult?

It's true: Some people just like the drama of a fight! They know what to say to piss you off. They want to fight with you. When this happens, you can choose not to fight. Try saying to yourself: "I'm here, I'm present; my presence means more than a fight." If it happens often, take the time to ask yourself if you really want to keep spending time with that person or group of people. The answer may be that it's not worth it!

I believe I have learned to become aware of these crazy behaviors in other people around me. I remind myself I do not have to be like them; I can walk away and keep choosing what is light for my family and me. Guess what? So can you!

Don't Move Too Fast

As I wrote this book, it became clear that I was moving too quickly with every person I was encountering. These new relationships were blissful at first…then; slowly, the abuse came like waves in the sea.

Be wary. Most victims have shown that they are "fixers"—finding solutions for everything that's wrong in an abusive relationship. Let go of the urge to fix others. Don't leave one abusive relationship for another.

Healthy Communication

A healthy relationship is all about respecting each other and the different things you need. Be sure to speak out about what you need calmly and clearly. This gives both you and the other person the chance to meet in the middle and compromise. Otherwise, no one will know how you really feel, you might resent the other person, and nothing will change. People can't guess what you need, tell them!

Be in touch with what you need, want, and share it with others. You have a right to the things you prefer, even if it is different from other peoples' opinions, needs or ways of doing things.

For example, my husband is deaf to some tones of voice. He tends to speak very loudly, all the time. I had to express to him that he needed to talk to me gently, not yell. I told him this is because the yelling brought back feelings of fear. Once he knew that this is what I needed and that it was important to me, he changed the way he spoke to me.

Don't let them judge you

"Let them misunderstand you. Let them gossip about you. Their opinions aren't your problems. You stay kind, committed to love and free in your authenticity. No matter what they do or say, don't you doubt your worth or the beauty of your truth. Just keep shining like you always do."
– Scott Stable

Final Note

Once you have the tools, what you do with them is up to you. I can sit here all day and give you recommendations about what works. But in the end, it's your choice.

Remember...

You are never alone. And it is never the end. Think about it, look back at all those similar unpleasant contexts where you fell prey to fear. If you are reading this now, then it wasn't the end, and chances are you were not alone either.

Once you come to grips with this realization, you can engage with challenges that life throws at you--it always does--from a much more resourceful space.

I have also learned on my journey; if not careful, I can still be taken advantage while desperately seeking and craving a healthy life and wanting to do better. I was able to fight through and triumph over most of the abuses; however, I was not prepared for the next abuse that I believe is the most horrible of them all.

THE ULTIMATE ABUSE

Consider this resume...

- Ordained as a priest since 1964
- 2x Author
- Catholic School Teacher
- Addicted to alcohol, left the church to turn his life around
- Went to school
- Licensed to practice Psychotherapy
- Known to have spiritual visions
- Endorsed by the Catholic Church

We all have chosen some dark paths, and God says if we are truly sorry and confess our sins, He will forgive us. As a Catholic, I was always taught if I sought our priest and made a confession I would be absolved of my sin. A strange twist occurred in of January of 2017 and continues to uproar as I share what took place. Sadly, it's something that I still deal with today although I try to erase it from my thoughts. In this book I talked about the different types of abuses and the possible solutions but what about 'Spiritual Abuse' from someone you believe God has called? 'Spiritual Abuse' happens when a spiritual authority; such as a cult or pastor who has special healings abuses and seeks to control individuals and ensure obedience.

Sometimes in seeking to become closer to the Lord and His power, we become vulnerable.

On January 31, 2017, I met with a laicized priest (a person endorsed to be a priest by the church but doesn't live under the church or a parish) who I was told had the miracle of healing in his hands. He was an author and someone who had a powerful testimony of what God did with his life. I made an appointment to meet him in his home located in Evangeline Parish.

A good friend of mine accompanied me to the appointment; she sat and waited patiently with me. I sat in silence waiting to be seen and listened to some ladies talk about the politics of Donald Trump. I remember the place smelling like someone passed away.

When I was called inside the room, the priest asked where I needed healing. I was having an issue within my cervix and was seeking relief from the pain. I laid down on the table in his office, and as he touched me, I felt like the Lord was healing me. I cried tears of joy. I surrendered to what I believed was the Holy Spirit and was in a trance by the prayers going forth. However, what I thought was a moment of healing and relief quickly turned into a moment of sexual abuse by way of inappropriate touching, choking and forcing me to participate with involuntary acts as I laid in a trance. Once coming to, he claimed this was his method of healing and encouraged me to come back for eight more visits, so I could be healed.

I was raised and still am a devout Catholic. While it took me some time to get to this point, I remember growing up and my grandmother having statutes of Mary everywhere. I learned that she is a saint, one of perfect servanthood and the mother of Jesus. I guess the priest could tell my dedication to God and my faith ran deep. He told me that Mary spoke to him concerning me and I should depend on him and him alone for healing. The priest told me that I had demons, which made me think something was wrong with me. However, how can that be true when I confessed my sins and knew I was forgiven. My mind and body screamed for me to run for my life. Don't look back!

I had to let the Catholic Church know about the person they endorsed. I had to share how this person took advantage of my belief when vulnerable. If he did it to me, I was sure this violation was done to others. To my heartbreak, the church did very little to support me or bring any disciplinary action on this person. I made the decision that I would not take this abuse as I endured in the past. I had to make a police report to bring charges.

With further investigation, I found a list of claims of abuse from this priest. With a resume like that, this priest was a fraud and a spiritual abuser who preyed on vulnerable women.

I believe the 'Spiritual Abuse' is the ultimate abuse because God is where we find our salvation, healing, and wholeness. It is through Him that we gain our strength to move forward and even share our stories. I believe it's important to understand that this type of abuse is very real, and we must be careful not to fall in. As you can imagine, I've been devastated by this ordeal, mostly, because I filed reports and alerted the church, and nothing has been done. I will continue to fight.

CONCLUSION

Remember at the beginning of this book I said, "Before we're born, God already has our life mapped out. However, once we get to a certain age of understanding who He is, we must also seek to find what He requires. Abuse is not of God! Abuse can only happen when the abuser chooses to turn away from God.

After some soul searching I have learned that God wants us to have normal relationships, recognize what is not of Him (abuse), learn to love ourselves, consistently evaluate our behavior and life (according to His word), make wise decisions (to help us, not to hinder or hurt ourselves), create plans (seek Him in the planning process), and seek peace (his peace).

It has taken me several years to learn and understand the 'Ugly Truth' about abuse. Now that I understand, I am on a mission to help women live their best lives that they can be proud of and where God would be pleased. Reader, will you help me to do that? You can start today by sharing this book.

Made in the USA
Columbia, SC
02 March 2019